Cosmo's War

SOLDIER, SON, ARTIST, BROTHER

GW00656392

A play about the power of letters

BERNARD ADAMS

© Bernard Adams/Annie Davis/James Clark Estate 2022

Published by F.S. & J. Rhys

ISBN 978-0-9539799-2-9

First Published August 2022

For Julia Rhys & Mona Adams

Two amazing women who had more than enough love, not just for their families, but also for the people and world around them.

Contents

STOP PRESS

The cruel folly of President Putin's invasion of the Ukraine is playing out on the streets of Kyiv as this book goes to press. *Cosmo's War* shows the agonising demands conflict makes on individuals, families and communities. Putin's War sadly indicates how much this book's message still needs to be propagated. In war individuals may survive – even thrive, often heroically – but every violent conflict always brings pain, causes misery and inflicts loss. War levels humanity down to a demeaning common denominator – survival.

Introduction

In 1915 John Cosmo Clark, a seventeen-year-old art student, volunteered to fight for his country. This account of his time in the trenches in France is told by a narrator and through his letters to his parents, his five brothers and sisters and theirs to him.

Volunteering had interrupted Cosmo's art studies, so at the front he began to sketch what he saw around him – sending the work back to Chiswick for comment by his art-teacher father. The exceptional wartime postal service did the rest.

Cosmo's War was originally performed as a rehearsed reading in Christ Church, East Sheen, London. The script which follows is the one used for that performance in 2018, but it can be adapted for a static reading, or for a fuller, costumed production with movement and as much realism as possible.

Performance

Cosmo's War can be seen as a play for reading or, more grandly, as an audio-visual documentary drama. The production in Christ Church, East Sheen, was somewhere between the two. Cosmo moved around the auditorium, went over the top (some chairs and a ladder), clambered onto his improvised hospital bed and, with marvellous dexterity, kept on reading from his script.

The play is, literally, a documentary. Every word spoken, other than by the Narrator, is taken from the marvellously preserved letters the family exchanged, detailing their deeply contrasted lives. To enhance the factual element in our production, visuals (as described in the text) were projected onto a modest screen. These included Cosmo's drawings done at the front, pictures of the damage caused by Zeppelin bombs falling on West London and images of Bedford Park. In future productions the visual ingredients could be more ambitious: for example, images from the rich store of WW1 stills and film could be projected on a large screen behind the players. Or we could follow, with the help of an animated on-screen map, Cosmo's tortuous progress through the killing fields of Flanders.

In our church production the drama of the piece was intensified by the vital audio element (admirably provided by Andy Hughes). Large loudspeakers delivered the deadly, deafening sounds of trench warfare. This realistic approach was effective, but a more imaginative, musical mode is possible – perhaps by moving away from realism and using percussion to create the sounds of the battlefield. Also, there is room to make more of the WW1 songs at the start and in the interval, and perhaps incidental music on the piano could be added at the more dramatic moments in the story.

The play is well suited to student productions and a small fee should be paid for copyright. The fee should be given to Combat Stress, the admirable charity which looks after veterans, or another suitable charity.

James Clark 1858 – 1943

Cosmo Clark's father, James, was a painter of quality. He was born in 1858 and lived in West Hartlepool for thirty years, building up a career as a versatile artist with a particular speciality in bible illustrations. He came to London in the 1880s with his growing family – living first in Chelsea and then moving to Bedford Park in 1914. He lived at 44 Rusthall Avenue until 1938.

When James began to get commissions for murals, he did them at home in Rusthall Avenue – in a studio far too small to accommodate huge paintings. He would stretch his canvas between two rollers – one on the floor and one on the ceiling, with a drawing board behind the canvas, from which he could copy his draft design which he had done in separate rectangles. Then the almost-finished canvas was stuck to a church wall – usually with white lead. In this photograph *(left)* he is on top of a rickety scaffolding in the church of St Barnabas in Ealing – putting the final touches to his work.

James Clark left behind a large body of work. He was especially good with children (he could catch their expressions and interactions with great skill) and families. He did excellent nudes, good portraits, fine still lives and vivid scenes of life in Palestine. He spent time there (1896-1897) to stock up on images for his bible illustrations.

During World War 1 when James's youngest son Cosmo grew bored with bouts of inaction in the trenches in France, he asked his father to send him drawing materials and he did so. The art student began to sketch again and James commented helpfully from Rusthall Avenue on the results. How the teenage artist/soldier managed after that is the subject of the play which follows.

"Greater love hath no man than this"   The Great S

The Great Sacrifice

At Christmas 1914 there was a terrible sense of shock in Britain. Battalions of young officers, the flower of the nation's youth, had fallen – leading their men into the early battles. Thousands would not return to their families for Christmas because they lay in improvised graves in Flanders. The nation was in bewildered mourning for its dead sons.

James Clark, who already had two sons in the Forces, and his youngest about to volunteer, caught the feeling of this moment perfectly in this painting – celebrating the selfless sacrifice of the young subaltern, with a ghostly Christ figure suggesting the possibility of an after-life. Clark himself called the picture 'Duty' *(left)* but when the illustrated weekly, The Graphic, published it as a Christmas colour supplement, they titled it, 'The Great Sacrifice'. 'In the history of nations nothing more glorious has ever been offered than this Great Sacrifice,' said the paper. Adding that they were offering 'the finest picture that this war has produced or is likely to produce'.

Millions of copies were sold, and the Graphic's colour supplement became so popular that newspaper stalls began to look like 'wayside shrines.' It cost the buyer one and fourpence, but Clark profited little from the picture's popularity because he gave it away for a charity sale. Queen Mary bought the original, and she graciously allowed James to make copies of it to order. So, Clark did a copy for Lord Aberdare – who had lost his son early on – with the fallen soldier now resembling the young Aberdare. There was also a demand from churches for stained-glass versions of the picture, which Clark fulfilled. For a few months he was perhaps the most famous painter in Britain.

Cosmo's War

Clockwise from top left: Cosmo, James Clark, Percy, Ruth, Ellen, Elizabeth (with granddaughter Elizabeth), Walter, Lilian, Little Cosmo (inset, Colville)

Characters

The parents:

James Clark painter and teacher

Elizabeth Clark mother of six

Their children:

Percy soldier and engineer

Colville naval officer

Cosmo subaltern (second Lieutenant)

Lilian curate's wife, mother of three

Ruth PE and dance teacher

Ellen trainee teacher

Additional character:

A prisoner facing a court-martial

17

Scene

A space with a platform for the seated readers. Eight chairs on raised area – one for each of the Clark family group. A separate position in the pulpit for the Narrator. The Clark parents and daughters remain in their 'home' behind the communion rail. They are in Chiswick while their sons and brothers are away at the war – in France or on the high seas.

The sons' chairs remain empty. Cosmo, Percy and Colville sit unobtrusively outside the communion rail until they speak, but later they sit, lie, lounge, stand, walk or even run as they read. Cosmo, in particular, moves around the auditorium freely.

There is a screen – above the family, centre-stage. At various points slides will appear. Actions will be devised for Cosmo and his brothers as they fight their battles and write their letters.

Costume

Appropriate 1915-1918 clothes may enhance the performance. Uniform for Cosmo is essential.

Props

Simple additions, like some knitting or darning for the mother, may be useful.

Act 1

For a few minutes before the speaking begins there is a medley of WW1 songs, played on the piano. The music should gradually hush the audience into silence as the lights fade and overlap the beginning of the pictures.

Stills: Edwardian Bedford Park – houses, church, the Tabard Pub etc.

Narrator

The model suburb of Bedford Park was added to Chiswick in the 1870s. From the start it was attractive to writers and artists. W.B. Yeats lived here for a time and so did Camille Pissaro.

Still: James Clark and family

Another painter, James Clark came to live with his family at 44 Rusthall Ave in 1914. At Christmas time in 1914 he suddenly achieved his moment of fame.

Still: The Great Sacrifice

He painted this picture, The Great Sacrifice, in response to the terrible – and unexpected – losses of young men in the early months of the Great War. A young soldier has died gallantly for his country. The picture offers solace; the youthful volunteer is not disfigured in death; it is almost as if he has fallen asleep. A ghostly, Christ-like figure offers comfort for the grieving relatives. The painting struck a chord – it appeared in many magazines and newspapers and distinguished people came to the Clark's house to see it – and some ordered another version of it, with the young officer clearly recognisable as their own son.

Still: Family group

Narrator

The artist was no bohemian Impressionist; James Clark was more a Victorian paterfamilias, a loving father with a family of six children. Originally, they had lived in Hartlepool in the North, but then came to London – at first to Chelsea and then to Bedford Park.

Still off

The family comes in, led by James. He sits in the central position behind the communion rail with Elizabeth.

These are the Clarks. There are only four of them – normally there would be eight, but six months into the war the family is very depleted. Let's introduce them.

James *(after this referred to as Father)*

Sorry to interrupt but I think in fact we can do the job very well ourselves, thank you: I am James Clark, a painter. I also teach at Goldsmiths' College, do murals in churches and create stained-glass windows. This is my wife…

Elizabeth *(after this referred to as Mother)*
Intervening quietly but firmly

My name is Elizabeth and I am the mother of six children. The house and home and the well-being of my family are my chief concern.

Lilian

As my brothers are away, I'd better be next. I'm Lilian the eldest. I'm married – to a curate – and have just had my third child. I live just a few doors away from my parents, in 28 Rusthall Avenue.

Indicating empty chair in the 'home'

My sister, Ruth…

Ruth

Speaking from stage right, outside the family circle

I'm working in Canada at the moment as a PE and dance teacher and wondering if I should come home to be with my family now that the war has started.

Ellen

Next to her parents, stage right

And I'm Ellen, the youngest daughter and I'm training to be an art teacher. I'm nearly qualified and hope I can get a job soon and support myself.

Narrator

All three of the boys are already away at the war: Percy is a sapper *(he comes forward and salutes)* and Colville is in the navy *(he salutes)*. Just recently, much to the parents' concern, their youngest son, the seventeen-year-old John Cosmo, abandoned art college and chose the Officers' Training Corps. *(He comes forward and salutes)* This is the story of Cosmo's, and his family's, war.

Cosmo could have stayed safely studying at his art

school, but he wanted to volunteer and so he joined the Middlesex regiment, The Diehards.

Earlier, he had tried to get into Percy's regiment as a motor-cycle dispatch rider. Percy wasn't keen.

Percy steps forward

Percy

It would be my job to order men to carry despatches to certain places and of course the jobs will be risky, and some will get killed. Well, it would be bad enough for me to think that the despatch rider was killed because he carried out my orders, but just imagine my feelings if the particular despatch rider that got killed or winged was my brother. I should never be able to forget it.

Narrator

Percy had already been commissioned in the Royal Engineers. He was writing from Aldershot, where he was engaged in a private war, with…

Percy

Lice, Lice, Lice – they are my enemy and I have been fighting them for two weeks now.

Much love to all from your affectionate brother Percy.

P.S. My enemies are not *on* myself.

Narrator

When his eighteenth birthday came around Cosmo was still with the Officers' Training Corps at Maidstone.

Cosmo is drilling

Mother

23 January 1915, Rusthall Avenue

My dear Cosmo,

This is to wish you many happy returns of your birthday and to bring you all the love it is possible to write. I do hope you are well; it was a great relief to me when Father came home and told us how comfortable your billet was and what a nice person Mrs Case is. I sent off a cake to you yesterday. I hope you got it today so that you can enjoy it tomorrow. So goodbye my dear son, heaps of love from everyone.

Always your loving mother, E Clark.

Ruth

From her remote position. Cosmo has stopped drilling and is reading his letters.

83 Simpson Street, Montreal

Many happy returns for your birthday and a great deal of love.

Cosmo opens a parcel and finds an enormously long scarf. He reacts.

This scarf is the result of my first knitting efforts. No doubt Mother and Ellen have provided you handsomely with comforters, socks and mitts, so do what you like with the scarf – give it to someone in your Corps or else to Percy for one of his men. I do hope you will get your commission, dear, we should be proud of our baby brother!

My love to all at home, and special birthday love to you. Ruth.

Father

13 February 1915, Rusthall Avenue

Cosmo, you should be reading and learning all you can about military duties. Getting a commission will depend on your efficiency in the OTC. Have a notebook and put down all you learn.

Much love my dear son, Father.

Ruth

3 May 1915, Montreal

Today I have heard about your commission and I am delighted and proud. You are awfully young in years to have such an enormous responsibility put upon you.

Father and mother seem anxious to have me home, and while the war is on and you boys serving, I feel that their wishes must guide me. But the idea of leaving here distresses me, I love the work, and the people I know, and the winter climate I adore. Indeed, only a sense of duty can make me give it up.

Always your loving sister, Ruth.

Ruth moves slowly to the empty chair in the bosom of the family.

Narrator

Soon after this letter, Ruth braved the U-boat infested Atlantic, where shipping losses were becoming alarming. The family suffered agonies while she crossed, but she arrived safely.

Cosmo

Dear Father,

Can you please let me have another sovereign? I am

very sorry to have to ask for more, but I have been as economical as possible. Paying the servant, together with washing, takes three and six away. For the past four days I have been in charge of C Company again, so have been very busy. We have been doing our firing at the long ranges. It's quite extraordinary how nervous a lot of the men are. Quite ten out of the whole two hundred and forty had to be coaxed and assured that everything was quite safe and that there was nothing to be afraid of about firing the rifle.

Ever yours cheerfully, Cosmo.

Narrator

The Clarks were a letter-writing family. The parents kept Cosmo informed about his sisters' activities and his brothers' progress in the services, and Cosmo's siblings wrote often to their little brother with news of their doings.

Ellen

14 July 1915

Have been to the dentist this afternoon and he fairly gave me gyp, just found the nerve and sat on it with the drill for about five minutes and then put something beastly hot into the hole – which put the cap on everything.

But now all pain has gone and as it had been aching all week, I think it was worth it. It's pouring with rain now and horribly miserable and, of course, I have just started a summery sketch in the garden and haven't had any sun since.

Mother

9 August 1915

This is just a line to let you know that Ellen has passed her exam. She is the only one from Goldsmith's College. We only heard by tonight's post and I know you will be very pleased about it as we all are here.

I will make your curtains and send them on very soon. Heaps of love, my dear Son.

Always your affectionate Mother, E Clark.

Father

26 September 1915

My dear Son, On Friday Colville telegraphed to say he was at once joining the yacht 'Zara'. It patrols the sea between the Scillies and Devonport. He thought it a fortunate appointment, while regretting his not spending this weekend with us. Percy's last letter told of time hanging heavily on hand – fortunately, we had sent him the fishing rod.

Affectionately yours, Father.

Mother

Colville's yacht, Zara, is owned by a Scotch millionaire and it is fitted up most gorgeously with every convenience, hot and cold water, electric light etc. so, as he puts it, they are living in the height of luxury. What a change for him after five years in a sailing ship. He says they will be at sea six days and in port two.

Narrator

By the middle of November 1915, 2nd Lieutenant Cosmo Clark was in Boulogne – although, because of censorship, he had to refer to it as 'a French seaport you will know.' The Middlesex men set off for the front in a horribly overcrowded train – the men standing up in cattle trucks – forty-four of them squeezed into each one. When they got to their destination, at one in the morning, Cosmo noticed some of the recruits could hardly stand up. And then they set off on a march which lasted till after 3.00am. Cosmo explained, in his exceptionally neat handwriting, what happened next.

Show Cosmo letter

Cosmo

My pack weighed quite a ton when we left the little French station and it increased in weight every half mile. It was a glorious night with a full moon, but jolly cold.

We arrived eventually at the little village where we are billeted at present. It's a very scattered, poor place – nearly every building is, or rather has been, a farm. After seeing the men of my platoon into their various barns – all lined with straw – I was told by my billeting officer: 'This is your billet – just go and knock them up – they're expecting you.'

Letter off screen

This is what I saw – a long, low house standing by itself, with just a few barns and outhouses tacked on. No lights anywhere (it was about four in the morning), about twelve doors and a good rich niff of 'cochons'. However, I waded through a sort of front garden and farmyard combined, and as I was very tired and didn't want to waste time, gave a hearty bang on one of the doors. Immediately about fifty dogs started barking, grunts came from the outhouses and jabbering from a female inside the house. Soon a door opened and a French madame, holding a candle, and in somewhat scanty attire, demanded if I was *'l'officier d'etre logé ici?'* I gave her a most emphatic *'oui'*, and she bade me enter in a very motherly way. I was agreeably surprised how well I got on with the lingo and soon we were best of friends.

Narrator

The scantily clad madame insisted on calling Cosmo *'Mon Brave'*, which embarrassed him somewhat. He was exhausted but he still had work to do – censoring about sixty of the men's letters home.

Cosmo

It was a queer job. Some were very funny and rather pathetic. They all start with: 'I hope this finds *you* as it leaves me – in the pink.' One man said he couldn't get any sleep 'because of the terrible roaring of the guns'. As a matter of fact, we can only just hear the faintest rumble.

My batman has just got my bath ready, so goodnight everybody and don't worry about me. I am as happy, comfortable and safe as possible.

Narrator

In the next few days more long marches took them to the area around Bethune.

Cosmo

On Monday when we were in our last village, Percy came over to see me – he's looking very fit and well. He came to our company mess and we all had a long talk. He seems to think that the Germans have shot their bolt and that the war will be over in about six months.

Saw a whole regiment of Scotchies coming back from the trenches to their billets this morning. They wore those tam o'shanter caps and though they were literally covered in mud, they all seemed cheerful enough. They remarked in passing: 'They are leading over there at half time by 1-0, go and have a shot at equalising it'.

Narrator

The chance to equalise the score didn't come for a while. But on 10 December, 1915, Cosmo wrote home saying that he had achieved…

Cosmo

My baptism of fire – as the papers like to call it. This morning I was sent in charge of a fatigue party of twenty-five men to our trenches to do some sandbagging. We were fortunate in seeing a most interesting artillery bombardment.

Bombardment. Cosmo looks up.

Our guns, which were of course behind us, were lobbing shells over our heads at a terrific rate. The Germans were returning our fire, but they didn't send half so many over as we did. You can always hear the shells coming, but you never can tell where they're going to drop! When you hear 'em coming the thing to do is to drop down and you're safe as houses.

Single shell burst

When a shell bursts, it bursts in an upward direction, so that if you are lying down only ten yards away the pieces go right over you. It's most interesting and infinitely more exciting than Salisbury Plain!

Narrator

Christmas 1915 came – the second of the war. No fraternisation this time; the heady days of the 1914 football match were over...

Cosmo

On Christmas Eve we spent most of the time buying things for the men. We subscribed altogether £10 which was spent on oranges, vegetables, chocolate, smokes and beer for our 250 men.

On Christmas Day we had a huge feed – turkey, plum pudding and all the usual etceteras – including hundreds of crackers. Afterwards we had a gramophone and dancing, singing and games. And we drank the king's health, which was a solemn proceeding. It seemed very funny to think that we were only two miles away from the Germans…

On Boxing Day, we went for a route march and then to the skating rink in the big town, commandeered for the 'resting' troops. Our band was playing, and we had a great time – I got on excellently and didn't fall down once.

Narrator

The Middlesex was still moving around to the north of Bethune. The rain and the icy mud were now beginning to get Cosmo down. On 1 February, 1916, he sent home this description of his quarters.

Cosmo

The dugout I'm in at present has the following dimensions – 14 foot long, 7 foot broad and 3 foot 6 inches high. Six of us live, eat and sleep here and we are none of us very small. Two are over six feet, so if you should want to move at all, everybody has to move at the same time… However, it has one consolation, it keeps us all warm, because for the last two days it has been very cold indeed.

Narrator

Next Cosmo went to the Givenchy sector of the line. In Boy's Own paper style, he wrote up his various adventures – including crawling through no-man's land with a lance-corporal, trying to find a German sniper who had been causing trouble. They eventually found him, calmly lighting a cigarette three hundred yards in front of his own lines. They noted his position, but then got horribly lost on the way back and for a while lay, completely confused, among the bodies of Canadians killed in an earlier battle. In the end they found their way home and the sniper was 'strafed.' Cosmo, however, had respect for the German soldier.

Cosmo

Can you believe the bravery of a man to wander out three hundred yards from his own men and snipe? I have a great admiration for that Bosch (that was).

On our part of the line where the trenches were close to the Huns, I actually *saw* my first German. The men told me that the Bosch were trying to fraternise with us. I went down and poked my nose around a traverse and there was a German, stripped to the waist and waving to me! I was jolly careful not to look for too long because they sometimes have another man training a rifle on you.

Soon he signalled to me to get down... I took the hint and sure enough some bombs came from where he had pointed. He was a Saxon, about twenty-three years old – clean shaven and with a trench cap on, the round soft cap which you have seen in the papers, and a grey uniform. He laughed at me when he was signalling... We shouted back to try to entice him to come over and give himself up, but he hadn't quite enough confidence in us.

Narrator

Because of the censor Cosmo's letters home were often guarded about place names and military details.

Cosmo

During our last time in the trenches, two Bosch gave themselves up to us. They were two hulking chaps, officers' servants, and because they had been maltreated, they had deserted – fetching with them a good supply of their officers' cigars, cigarettes and wine – in sandbags.

Narrator

By March 1916 Cosmo's regiment was still circling Bethune. As the waiting became more and more tiresome, Cosmo's thoughts turned back to his disrupted education. So, he started sketching and sending the results home for appraisal...

by his father. Although the family was being disturbed by Zeppelin raids on London, James Clark sent his comments and did his best to have his son's drawings published.

Father

I went to the Graphic office with your sketches, but Mr Pasquier wasn't in. The last batch of your sketches continue the standard of their predecessors. The single heads were somewhat better.

Sketches off

Cosmo

Dear Mother and Father

Father asks in his letter why it is that the dangers, or rather the various killing schemes of the Bosch, are always referred to in a joking manner. It's the only way to look upon these things. Often, when deep down in your heart, you have a terrible fear of them, you can pass it off and get over it quickly by joking about it. If it wasn't for the light-hearted way in which the British Army takes these things, half of 'em would be sent home with 'nerves.' (*Sighs*) More than four months away from home is more than enough to make me realise what a pleasure home is.

Father

9 April 1916

My dear son

We're all hoping you may arrive on your leave before Percy goes back from us.

More sketches on

I have heard no further yet from Pasquier about the drawings – he is evidently not finding it easy to work them in. I much liked your bombing subject, by the way.

Sketches off

The German Imperial Chancellor's speech to the world was this week's sensation. The most colossal lying one could possibly conceive. And he evidently thinks it will be accepted.

Always affectionately yours, Father.

Narrator

In May 1916, Cosmo came back to France after a short, blissful leave at home and was wounded almost immediately.

Sudden loud shell explosion

Cosmo

Just a bit of shrapnel in the Gluteus Maximus. Nothing serious. When I was hit, I was no good up in the line because it hurt me a bit to walk, and also, I was a bit shaken. It was a large 5.9 shell which came amongst a party of us who were repairing a trench just by the village school. Of course, the explosion was terrific and the force of it knocked us over and over. Bricks fell and the dust and smoke were so thick you couldn't see. When we picked ourselves up and started feeling various parts of us to see if we were still there, we found that there was only me and another man hit. We both went down to the dressing station and from there to the Field ambulance. However, the main thing is that I'm fit as a flea now and none the worse for my experience. It has surprised me how very close a big thing can burst without hurting you. The post-corporal is here so I must close.

With best love, Cosmo.

Narrator

Cosmo was soon back in action – at Vimy ridge where he was involved in a ferocious artillery battle.

Cosmo

At four o'clock our guns started an intense bombardment.

Intense bombardment, continues throughout this speech

Never have I experienced such a time. There was the long continuous scream and groan of our shells whistling over our heads and a continuous roar as they exploded in the German trenches. This kept on till 8.30 in the evening. Although one wasn't actually frightened, the everlasting roar and scream made everybody literally tremble with anticipation and excitement. The Germans retaliated but they gave us far less than we gave them. At eight thirty our mines went up and I had a splendid view of them. They don't make much noise, but they make the ground rock backwards and forwards for a good half-minute. All you can see of the explosion is an immense tongue of flame about twice the size of our house. Great chunks of earth flew into the air like so much paper, as did some old Bosch, spread-eagled against the sky.

Bombardment dies down

Narrator

But there were quiet days and nights as well.

Cosmo

17 May 1916

I was on duty from 1.00am till stand-to which is about 2.30am just now. During all this time, except for an occasional shot, all was absolutely quiet. It was a beautiful night – warm, still and a full moon in a cloudless sky. All I had to do was to walk up and down our company front, asking each sentry as I passed him if all was quiet. A boring job to say the least of it. The Bosch are about three hundred yards away from where we are at present. We could hear them singing and shouting occasionally. In turns, star shells would be fired to assist the moon in lighting up no-man's-land, with its rows and rows of barbed wire.

Narrator

Peaceful nights soon came to an end; the great Somme offensive had begun.

Father

16 July 1916, Rusthall Avenue

My dear son

Every morning and evening the newspapers are sold like wildfires spreading quickly. The work at Contalmaison and thereabouts is followed yard-by-yard. The daily lists of rolls of honour are sad but show how our amateur armies can face death like the best in Europe.

Mother and I calculate that you have again, a day or two ago, started a turn in the trenches. *Bon courage!*

Much love my dear son,

Affectionately yours, Father.

Ruth

We are not glad to hear you are going into such a hot bit of the line. Thank God you had the grit to join the army in time to be ready when you were wanted.

I have been away for five days to Faygate in Sussex – it's not many miles from Horsham and the country around is most lovely – small private woods (where one is allowed to wander) opening out into such heavenly open country with far-off hilly views.

Father says to tell you to wear your steel waistcoat if you are able. Father and Mother send much love, as I do.

Ever your loving sister, Ruth.

Cosmo

My dear Mother and Father

You *must not* worry so much about me. I know you are sure

to worry a lot, but everybody has a jolly good chance out here and the number of days one isn't in the danger zone greatly exceeds the number one is.

Narrator

Cosmo was about to enter a danger zone where he would *not* have 'a jolly good chance.' In the great Somme battle tens of thousands of men had already been lost in gaining just few yards of ground.

Cosmo

I've just been with Elliott and Henderson…

Narrator

Fellow officers…

Cosmo

…having a good look at the German prisoners who were working hard close to here under the sharp eyes of several French tommies. Really, although one is naturally set against the Bosch as a whole, I've never in all my life seen such…

Pictures of German captives

…a lot of savage, cruel-looking brutes huddled together. I can never expect mercy from men of their type, and you can take it from me if I ever have the chance, they'll get none from me. They looked as if they couldn't stick together under a bombardment except by being bullied. A miserable, demoralised-looking lot of swines. Enough!

Captives pictures off

By bye, best of love to all, ever your affectionate son, Cosmo.

Father

Cosmo,

Vile as most of the Germans have proved themselves to be, I cannot imagine an Englishman killing one who is in terror and offering himself as a prisoner, unless he had seen the same German treacherously murder a comrade. We must not let the war make us as bad as they are. Naturally after one of our terrific bombardments the prisoners taken are in an awful state of collapse… The photographs I most dislike to see are huge groups of laughing and leering men waving and holding trophies of the slain enemy. How can they? I can understand the awful duty of exterminating the enemy, or dying in the attempt, but not joking, leering, sneering afterwards.

Narrator

The slaughter at the Somme continued week after week.

In late July Cosmo told his parents he was in a huge valley packed with transport and cavalry.

Cosmo

The weather is beautiful, and we are all going for a bathe in the river which has figured so much in the papers lately… When it's lovely weather like this and everybody is well, one can't feel down in the dumps – what a wonderful thing sunshine is!

Cosmo watercolour

I got another watercolour finished which I am sending home. I hope it arrives on time. Will you let me know what you think of it please? It's a new kind of composition for me and I don't know whether it's good, bad, indifferent – or rotten.

Father

Your last watercolour sketch hasn't arrived yet, I do hope it turns up eventually.

More sketches

In sketches of things that impressed you, trust your intuitions, don't be hampered by how you *think* you ought to do it – if you can but realise what you wish to express, do it anyhow. How queer to be writing of art when there are such mighty events moving!

Sketches off

Love, prayers and continual well-wishing my very dear son, from your affectionate Father

During the Narrator's next speech, the 'front' is fixed in place

Narrator

At the beginning of August 1916, Cosmo was recommended for a captaincy. His moment at the Battle of the Somme was about to come. Already morale had been dented.

Cosmo

2 August 1916

I am commanding C Company – Elliott went down with shell-shock – he was a very highly strung chap and couldn't stand it; he was absolutely a mad lunatic when he came back. His is not the only case, so you can get some idea of what the shellfire was like. Now everybody's nerves are in a rotten state and the responsibility of the company is in my hands; living with nobody but 'nervy' people isn't strengthening *my* nerve! It's the reaction to it all – men who are as callous as could be usually, are now ducking down when our own guns are fired.

It is wonderful, when one is in perfectly hellish circumstances out here, with great responsibilities on one's shoulders, how the only comfort one can get is in prayer. It proves without doubt that, whatever is happening, there is always a Great Helper watching over one. If anybody who says there is no God could come out here and see literally hundreds of men instinctively turning to a Great Almighty for help, they would soon alter their opinion.

Cosmo begins to climb up the side of the trench – ready to go over the top

Ellen

Hadfield Road, Margate

I hear that you are now in command of C Company Let's hope you don't see too much fighting, or if you do, that all will go well – though a nice, cushy Blighty one would be rather a relief just now, wouldn't it? We are all having a very jolly time down here – quiet but perfect weather and bathing.

Narrator

The Somme offensive continued relentlessly, despite the losses. On Tuesday, August 8, 1916, acting-captain Cosmo Clark led his men over the top at 4.00am

Cosmo goes over the top and when he lands there is a sudden loud shell explosion – then a blackout. Cosmo crawls to a resting place. Heavy shellfire continues.

By 3.00pm on the same day, he was writing home

Cosmo

My dear Mother and Father

I do hope my post card and this letter arrive home before any wretched telegram from the War Office. I was wounded at 4.00 this morning when my Company and Captain Salter's made an attack. The wound is not serious at all, but during these times I believe it's bad enough to get me home.

Heavy shellfire

We had between four and five hundred yards to attack over and all this intervening ground was a perfect blaze of heavy shellfire. I got hit at the back of my thigh by a piece of shell – just above the back of my knee.

I was about half-way across when I got winged and I manged to keep on for a little while with the men before it gave out.

He has been crawling towards the 'bed'. When he arrives shellfire fades.

The bone isn't broken – it's only a flesh wound and not very painful. I haven't been sent to the base yet, but I expect to be, either today or tomorrow. At present I'm lying in a bed in a very big hospital that's *right-away-from-the-shells.*

All the wounded officers are discussing their chances of being sent to Blighty. I'll write again tomorrow. Don't worry.

Best love to all, ever your affectionate son, Cosmo.

Father

My very dear son

After the anxiety of the last few days it is almost a relief to get the official telegram saying you were 'admitted to No 20 General Hospital, Carnières, 9 August with gunshot wound, left thigh and back – slight'. How thankful we are for that word 'slight'. May God bless and heal all your troubles soon. We long to hear from you.

Always your affectionate Father.

Mother

We do sincerely trust the wound is 'slight.' Will you be sent to England? I do hope so – where you may get a long rest. I wish I could be near you just now.

Best love, we pray that you may be soon restored.

All my love, Mother

Cosmo

In spite of the fact that I have got a piece in my leg, I am *not* for Blighty! I was to have been operated on to extract the piece, but the doctors have consulted, and this morning told me that as it was so small, they were going to leave it. It would mean making a big hole in my leg – which they didn't feel justified in doing. I only wish they would fish for it and send me home.

Pause, gets out of bed, sits and delivers this intense message

Now to business. To be perfectly candid I want to tell you that, after what we've been through during the last fortnight, I feel that I simply cannot stick the infantry much longer. I should think I've seen a thousand mangled corpses lately – besides various worse sights and very few of the original battalion are left – only three of the original officers. Soldiering with strange officers and men is not enjoyable.

Ruth

16 August, Margate

Three letters came from you today with the very

disappointing news that you are not for Blighty. I think I can a little bit understand your horror of the going back – your description of the action was hell, so to go back into it needs a very heroic man. But you know, dear, that even small horrors are more difficult to bear when one's nerves are out of order and real, awful, ones must be proportionately increased. Do try and live one day at a time and accept the ease and comfort and rest of the hospital, without thinking of the future.

Narrator

Cosmo, in this apparently uncensored letter, explained why he felt he couldn't go back to the trenches.

Cosmo

I think I never told you what happened when we attacked the wretched Hun. At four o'clock in the morning of the 8th you will see in the papers we attacked Guillemont – our battalion were just on the left, holding Waterloo farm, and on our immediate left was Delville Wood. I think these three places are the most terribly awful spots in the whole world. The sights one sees are like the most dreadful nightmares and life up there *is* a nightmare. Nothing but death and horrors everywhere. At night when you're being shelled you can hear the wounded fellows crying out where you can't get to them; and when you do try, you can't get them to the Aid post because of the hellish fire. The stench is awful because of this boiling hot weather we've been having. Dead men, friend and foe, lie about in heaps often with their wild, grinning faces turned to you, others sleeping peacefully. Perhaps I shouldn't have told you all this, but I expect you now understand why we all think the life of an infantryman a hard one and why he thirsts to get away from it.

If I can get into something less aggressive, I should prefer it – more especially, if it would be somewhere where I could do more drawing. It's two years now since I left it and it will need all my time to make it up. Just think how splendid it would be for me to get some regular drawing every day. I long for it.

Narrator

The obvious place where Cosmo could achieve this was in the 'Disguising Corps' which designed camouflage for the army. His father said he would get in touch with the man in charge, a Mr Soloman.

Father

I will do all in my power to get you a change of work. I haven't the slightest doubt that in a week or two you will feel equal to anything again. It is most natural, a common experience, that the horrors and terrors should un-nerve for a while. Cheerful companionship and prayer, with restored health, will work wonders. Much love, my dear boy. I know God is caring for you in answer to our prayers.

Ruth

I hope very much indeed that you will get a move into the Disguising Corps – you surely should, for you have done your whack in the infantry. But try not to think at all and if you have to go back you will find that after your nerves have recovered, it will be easier than you suppose now, and you will be given strength to do it.

Narrator

The Clark family was dispersed in that summer of 1916 – James was in Wales, painting, and most of the rest were enjoying the beach at Margate where Lilian had brought her three young children and had the support of her mother, her two sisters and her husband John. This gave her time to write a rare letter.

Lilian

Hatfield House, Margate

My dear Cosmo

I can't say I am sorry that you are safely tucked up in

bed, away from those awful shells. I am quite sure you are glad to be having this rest and we are truly thankful your wound is not serious. You can't wish more than we do, dear laddie, that you may be sent home on sick leave.

John got a splendid lot of prawns tonight – off the rocks, about a quart – real prawns, such as you see sticking in lemons in the fishmonger's shops – what luxury for breakfast and in wartime too!!

Everyone is talking, so it is rather difficult to write. Ellen and mother have been to a concert; the baby has been very naughty about going to sleep but sleeps well when she goes off. The boys are awfully good and look so bonny and brown… Our very best love; rest all you can.

God bless you, ever your affectionate sister, Lilian.

Narrator

Despite all this support and encouragement, Cosmo would have found it difficult to go back into battle straight away. But then he had a stroke of luck; without knowing it, he had been incubating trench fever and, in September 1916, he was sent home to be treated in the London Hospital. Trench fever is spread by lice – Percy's old Aldershot enemy and now Cosmo's.

Pause

James Clark had made little progress with his efforts to get his son into the 'Disguising Corps', but Cosmo was now able to recuperate away from the guns. Then came some cheering news.

Cosmo

12 September 1916, George Ward, The London Hospital, Whitechapel E.

You probably saw in the papers that I was gazetted Captain with seniority from 22 June. I am very bucked about it.

Narrator

Captain Cosmo Clark was still only nineteen. As he rested and reflected, he didn't know whether he would have the strength to return to the infantry. Could he face the nightmare battlefields of the Somme again? Could he regain – and hold – his nerve? And, if he did, would he, along with millions of others...

Still: *The Great Sacrifice*

become one more victim of The Great Sacrifice?

Piano: *Short chorus 'Keep the Home Fires Burning*

Interval

CAFÉ
LION
D'OR

Jolly Cold Day

THE MITRAILLEUSE EMPLACEMENT
CALLONÉ, MARCH 1916.

Daybreak

C Coy Killed in Action.

"NO COMPRIS MADAME"

Feb. 19..

Act 2

Short musical introduction – perhaps the same song as was used before the interval

Scene

The same as Act 1 – except that the 'Front' has now moved further back in the church.

Narrator

By the spring of 1917 Cosmo was feeling better. Rest had restored him, and he was back with his regiment, training in England and doing massive amounts of administration. The Disguising Corps option seems to have been forgotten and he was prepared to take his chance as an infantryman once more. At least the Allies had made *some* progress: the line had now advanced a dozen miles towards Germany, but at a terrible cost in lives.

Percy

31 April, BEF France

My dear Cosmo

Thanks awfully for your letter. If it can possibly be worked, I intend to try and get away for 10 days this summer. It would be splendid if we could get away together. You talk of the monotony of life in England. Well, try and cast your mind back to when you were here!

I am convinced that life will only be enjoyable when this show is over. In the meantime, I think a quiet rest with the family down by the sea is the nearest approach to happiness we can get. Ten days of bathing, fishing and slacking is what I most want. It's three years since I had such a rest.

So long old son, yours ever, Percy.

Narrator

Earlier Cosmo had been corresponding with his other brother, Colville. While he was on leave, Cosmo had taken on… kindly, but perhaps rashly, the task of doing a drawing of Colville's girlfriend Doris.

Colville

Dear Cosmo

Do be prepared for a blow right from the chest – namely the drawing arrived quite safely and thanks for taking the trouble to do it, but unfortunately the likeness, to put it mildly, is off, or in plain English, rotten. I am frightfully disappointed as I thought you were sure to get the right thing.

Narrator

Cosmo cannot have been pleased with this reaction to his work, but he seems to have kept his cool and sent some photos which he had taken when he was visiting Colville in Belfast.

Colville

I think they are all excellent and quite the best I have seen of Doris. Can you see I am always anxious to have anything to remind me of my best beloved? When you can't see the real thing, a good photograph is a great thing to have. Cosmo, don't go and get drafted over to France or anything rotten like that; try and show them what a good hand you are over this side.

Cheer oh, Colville.

Narrator

Colville's naval job was stressful – sailing around the North Atlantic, doing reconnaissance.

Naval explosions

Colville

We all but pushed over a couple of mines a few days ago and also heard a sub. The panic that ensued was wonderful; you never saw anything so humorous. Aren't the shipping losses tremendous? They are playing the devil with us. We shall be jolly hungry in a month or two at this rate and I fail to see how much longer we can go on. Write when you have a few minutes to spare.

Yours, Colville

Narrator

By 9 August 1917 Cosmo was back in France, where the front had moved a dozen or so miles north from the Somme. He was in comfortable quarters and battle-ready once more – he hoped. But he would have preferred to be on a sketching holiday in Wales with Lilian and his father and mother.

Mother

August 23rd, Cwymbychan Bach, North Wales.

My dearest son

Here we are among the most wonderful and lovely scenery with mountains and hills all around us. Ruth sent on your letter written in the trenches. It was reassuring to hear you are in a fairly quiet place. Father has quite a good studio here in one of the granaries – with a small top light. He is feeling much better, but he had a very bad turn and for some days was very poorly. However, I feel sure the change up here will do him a lot of good. Goodnight my very dear son, heaps of love and all good wishes.

God bless and keep you safe.

Always your loving mother, E.Clark

Father

29 August 1917, North Wales

My dear son

So, you were sent to the front line straight away – it was perhaps just as well to get the plunge over.

Bon courage – and keep lying low till you learn all the newest Bosch dodges.

Father.

Narrator

Back in Rusthall Avenue after the holiday, Lilian confided to her young brother how much she wanted to be more than just a housewife and mother.

Lilian

Father's criticism of my sketches was *so* encouraging; he said I had advanced a lot and I must try to keep up my work – I can tell you this praise was sweet music to my ears. Because of attending to home duties I have let it drop so much (it's over three years since I did any landscapes) that I was quite sure that I had lost all I knew. You don't know how often I feel inclined to let the house and children go, and work at my painting. But I can't – only because I can't live in a mess, like the Muckles. But the conditions of work in Wales, the inspiring surroundings, exhilarating air and the elusiveness of the subjects got hold of me and I never enjoyed my work so much or felt so confident.

Best love from us all, ever yours, Lilian.

Cosmo

20 September

Last Monday the Colonel let me go off on my horse to meet Percy. I had a lovely ride across country to the village. Percy arrived at about 12 o'clock. He looks very fit but has only just got over his dose of gassing. The chief effect it had was to upset his digestion. I had about an hour with him and then he had to go off in his car.

Narrator

Soon afterwards the brothers took a trip together to Paris where they ate very well, enjoyed people-watching from cafes and marvelled at the hell-for-leather motor traffic. Back in Chiswick, Zeppelins had been making life unpleasant.

Lilian

We are thankful to have a rest from the raids. They have been far too numerous, although I have got past the stage of being nervous. I am only anxious till the children are safe downstairs. The last raids lasted so long (the guns were booming for two and a half hours one night) and the children lost so much sleep that I put up camp beds for them downstairs, so they need not be disturbed. They thought it great fun to be sleeping on 'soldiers' beds' (one was yours) in the studio. They are back upstairs since the moon has waned and the wind and rain came.

Best love from all of us, ever yours affectionately, Lilian.

Ruth

44 Rusthall Avenue

No doubt you have heard of our taste of war! Bad enough for us to realise a little bit what life in France must be like and to make us wonder how you can stand it. Mercifully none of us suffer from 'nerves' and indeed I've not come across many people who show signs of fear, but one feels the effects somehow – I find that we are limp the next day. Saturday was our worst night. Shrapnel did damage to streets between here and the High Road, where people were hurt enough to go to hospital.

Such numbers of people have come out to stay in Richmond and Ealing… The part I mind is that the result of the extra population is that always the trains are so packed that it is just ghastly getting to and from college. I am far less frightened of the raids than I am of the crush in the trains, or the possibility of disease from being in those crowds.

Good night. Ever yours lovingly, Ruth.

Narrator

Her mother is busy, and mostly cheerful, but even she is getting war-weary.

Mother

Now if only this war was over and you were back home, what a lot we could do and what a change it would be for us all – instead of thinking, as we do, of nothing but the war. It will be difficult to realise what peace will be like, after three years of frightfulness.

Narrator

James consumed the newspapers for war news relentlessly.

Father

We are delighted your company came through the attack so well. What a dreadful time they are having fighting towards Passchendale Ridge… We saw photographs of the kind of ground they have to cross. No shelter from fire, except in a cold bath of mud. Their achievements are marvellous, incredible.

Narrator

Then something cheerful happened. Colville got married to his Doris. Cosmo couldn't get away from the Front to be there, but Colville sent him a glowing account of the big day.

Colville speaks from within the family unit – behind the communion rail.

Colville

15 November

Dear Cosmo,

Many thanks for the letter and all the good wishes you sent with it. What a miserable shame that you were not over here, then it would have been quite complete. Of course, you were going to be 'best man'…

Well, it wasn't half so bad as I expected – in fact I was just beginning to enjoy it when it came to an end. In spite of the fact that the ring got stuck on the second joint and all the pushing and shoving in the world would not send it home, everything went off OK.

Of course, there were old boots by the score, not to mention empty petrol tins, tied to the back of the taxi. After a very nice lunch we pushed off, nobody knowing where we were bound for, but as a matter of fact we thought it wisest to stay in London that night, so booked up at the Kenilworth in Great Russell Street.

We had dinner and imagine our horror and surprise, on leaving the table, to find two little patches of confetti under each chair – and us both trying to look as though we had been married all our lives!

Well son, news is scarce so I must close, but if you want to know where to find perfect happiness and joy, find the right girl and marry her.

Cheer oh, ever yours, Colville.

Narrator

More confidences came Cosmo's way in a frank letter from his oldest brother who had been in England.

Percy

26 November, France

I was glad to get your letter. I have just got back from a course on wireless. On the whole, I had a good time there. Miss Baker is in the South African hospital in the town, and after braving the Matron and, getting the necessary permission, I called and two little dinner parties for two, and one or two little teas, resulted. I don't know what your opinion is, but I think she is very little to rave about, except a pretty face and a good figure.

You, in common with other members of the family, seem very keen on me marrying. So far, your hopes have nothing to justify them. I think it is extremely unlikely that I shall ever get married for the simple reason that this war will go on for some years yet, and short spasms of leave in England to satisfy one's desires and months of boredom in this country – punctuated by moments of intense fright – are not conducive to a state of mind where one welcomes or longs for married bliss.

Cosmo, I am beastly fed up. I am contemplating a change. I have got to the point now when I fail to take any interest in my work. In fact, I am smelling out a job as Officer Commanding Signals, Tanks. As far as I can make out it's the one branch of the service where one can run one's show without hindrance.

This is a miserable sort of letter, but I have fairly got the hump. It's my liver, I think.

We are still in the same place, so drop in and see me.

Yours ever, Percy.

Narrator

Cosmo was now relatively comfortable in a quiet part of the line.

Cosmo

We are in tents in a thick wood and jolly well off. It is very interesting making yourself comfortable for the nights –

out of odd bits of material. Everybody sets out to find what they can. My servant found a spring mattress for me out of a ruined house and has covered it with clean canvas. I hope it isn't lousy though; it is quite likely to be because the old Hun hasn't long left this place.

Biscuit tins to wash in tomorrow. Stoves out of the ruined houses to keep the tent warm. Piles of wood from the forest to keep the fires going. Chairs from the ruined houses. It's great fun pinching all you can. The great thing is to get there first.

Narrator

Back in Chiswick James Clark was feeling reflective and his wife proud.

Sound of Zeppelin raid and pictures

Father

Over three years a soldier now, my son; you will bear its impress all your life, whatever you become. This brutal struggle cannot go on for ever! Even now the Germans would accept a compromise they little dreamt of two years ago. But what a failure that would be from our point of view – the wild beast left to heal his wounds and attack the world.

Mother

16 December 1917

My dearest son

I don't give up hope that soon you may get your leave and be home with us again. How splendid it would be if we had you for Christmas.

The church pictures are going to be a huge success. Father has never done such good work as he is doing now; I know you will think the same when you see these pictures. Goodnight my very dear son, very best love and every good wish.

Always your loving mother, E Clark.

Ruth

20 December

My dearest Cosmo

We are all still hoping that you will turn up, smiling for Christmas Day.

Baby Cosmo has got the measles! Isn't it rotten luck? We were looking forward to the children this Christmas and now we are done out of it. It is such a glee to watch those infants undoing parcels and finding 'exactly what I wanted'.

A great deal of love and ever so many good wishes to you from your very loving sister, Ruth.

Lilian

I am writing your Christmas letter in the nursery, with a very measly little Cosmo in bed; he feels so much better today now that the rash is out. The other two are still about; we have not attempted to isolate them as the doctor says it is useless. We are all very disappointed at not being able to go to Grandma's for Christmas and I know they will miss us very much.

We have had no end of good things in presents – from Ipswich a chicken and new-laid eggs, a sack full of potatoes from Annie, cake from Dorie. John…

Narrator

Her husband…

Lilian

…got an afternoon's shooting last weekend and returned with a rabbit and a pheasant of his own killing and a bag full of apples. A letter from Uncle Lauritz…

Narrator

who owns the farm where they stay in North Wales…

Lilian

…says he is sending a goose, so altogether we have been most fortunate, as there is more or less a famine in meat. This morning I stood in a margarine queue for one and a half hours. I was there by 7.45 and got served a quarter of an hour after the shop opened at nine. At that hour there was a line nearly 200 yards long, people standing four or five deep.

I wonder how you will spend Christmas day? Not in the trenches, I hope.

Narrator

Miraculously that year Cosmo *did* get some leave from the trenches, and he was able to spend Christmas 1917 in the bosom of his family. Afterwards he returned to bitter weather in the Hargicourt sector of the line. In his cold hut, with sleet falling, he says, 'Oh! For my bed in Rusthall Avenue.'

Ellen

17 January 1918, Bristol

This is to congratulate you on your coming of age. Many happy returns for the day – the birthday of course, not the sort of day you will be having this birthday. Since I came back to this comfortless place on Monday…

Narrator

The school she taught at in Bristol…

Ellen

…it has snowed unceasingly – wet, sloshy snow. The students were to arrive yesterday but only about half turned up because some of the stations were completely snowed up.

Mother

My dearest son

This letter ought to reach you about the 24th and it brings ever so much love, along with many happy returns for your birthday. It hardly seems possible that it is twenty-one years since I first gazed on your dear little face lying close beside me. I was a proud mother then, but not more proud than I am now of my brave boy.

Narrator

Ruth was now working at the Chelsea College of Physical Education and she kept Cosmo informed about their parents.

Ruth

12 February

Daddy is so much better. It is most marked; he looks better and is quite his old self to live with again. Mother too is well and so wonderfully patient and unselfish amidst all the inconveniences of life – I get fed up and annoyed, but she just goes on without a murmur, except to rail against the people who grouch about the things they can't have instead of making the best of what they *can* have!

Cosmo

16 February 1918, France

The sun has been shining continuously since half-past eight this morning onto quite beautiful country of rolling hills with the ruined carcasses of villages dotted about among the valleys.

My company is in support and my headquarters, in which I am now writing, is about forty-five feet below the ground. In consequence we are proof against any kind of shell. All day we dig trenches and put up barbed wire at night ready for old Hun, should he attempt his long-boasted stunt.

Narrator

In England the press was predicting an imminent German attack – the 'long-boasted stunt.' The Germans had won their war with Russia, so more troops were available to fight on the Western Front. At Rusthall Avenue James was full of family concerns: he was worried about his eldest daughter. She has three children under five; and her husband John is away a great deal, sometimes in France, lecturing.

Father

Lilian is 'run down', thin, overworked and worried. I think the wife of a poor man…

Narrator

Poor because he was a curate…

Father

…who has even a small family, has the hardest and dreariest life of any in the community. Poor things, like those joining the army or going to sea, they little know the trials in store for them when they marry.

Cosmo

March 1918, France

The possible German offensive appears to be discussed

more in the newspapers than by the soldiers out here. Football and games seem to interest them much more. I took part in a battalion cross-country race of three and a half miles. I was surprised to find how much more difficult it sounds than it really is.

Sound of a WW1 era foxtrot

We get all the up-to-date theatre music in the mess. The dances we have in the evenings are great sport. Tell Ruth I can remember five fox-trot steps which isn't bad considering there are about fifty in all.

Narrator

But soon Cosmo wouldn't have much more time to perfect his fox-trot.

Fox-trot fades

He managed a meeting with Percy who told him, 'brother to brother', that a German offensive *would* begin in a few days' time. On 21 March Ludendorf's huge attack started with the heaviest bombardment of the whole war. The battles which followed were written up by Cosmo – his diary of the Somme Retreat. There was so much movement over the next ten momentous days that all communication with his family was cut off.

Narrator

Diary: 21 March 1918

Huge bombardment

Cosmo

I was awakened at 4.00am by a terrific enemy bombardment. I got up and dressed, as did all the other officers. At 4.20 the order came round to "stand by". At 4.45 the battalion was ready to move. At 4.50am we received the order to man our battle position. After the usual hustle and bustle in the early morning, my Company was ready. The thick mist made it rather difficult for me to find the way as we marched up to our battle position.

Gas sirens

After marching about half a mile, we heard the gas sirens and horns in front, hooting hard. About the same time, we could faintly smell the gas – not strongly but sufficiently so to make me order gas masks to be readied.

Two miles along the road, I had to cut across country to our positions. The fog up there was even denser and I had to use my prismatic compass and count my steps to ensure a correct direction for guiding the Company.

Eventually we arrived at our battle positions. Both the

thick mist and the intense bombardment continued. At 1.20pm the mist lifted, and the sun came out. I was extremely grateful for this because I could get a better view of what was going on in front of me. German aeroplanes were very active.

Aeroplanes

What little news I gained during the day came from the wounded coming back from the front line.

Narrator

By the spring of 1918 the Germans knew that if they were going to win the war they needed to do it quickly because the Allied blockade was beginning to starve them of food, and the Americans were about to throw in their soldiers on the Allied side. At first General Ludendorf's attack was successful and many of the British front-line defensive redoubts surrendered.

Shellfire, then machine guns

Cosmo

Diary, 22 March 1918

At 9.30am I learnt that the other two Companies of the battalion, who were in similar redoubts to ours, but about 1000 yards in front, were fighting hard – as they now constituted our front line. At 11.30 the mist cleared, and I could see the enemy barrage on our front line. By this time our positions were being heavily shelled with 5.9s, though there were no direct hits on our trenches. At 1.00, after a quick lunch of cold beef and bread, I observed the remains of our front line retiring from their position back towards our lines, and also numerous German machine gun teams following them up and inflicting casualties on our fellows as they fell back, fighting. Our men were able to open fire and help to cover the retirement.

While the men were engaging the enemy, I got my four subaltern officers together. My orders were to hold on at all costs, and so we shook hands on it, and quite thought that our last day on this earth had arrived. This practice became quite common in the ensuing days.

Narrator

Suddenly a static war had become a war of movement – almost all of it in the wrong direction for the Middlesex men.

Aeroplane attack

Cosmo

Four German aeroplanes suddenly swooped down and peppered us with their machine guns, killing three of my men. I got a Lewis gun onto them as quickly as possible, but they were off in no time.

I then found the Colonel and got orders to march back to the cross-roads south of Merancourt. We found a tent encampment waiting for us there with the Company Cookers ready with hot tea. I went straight to bed and slept like a top till 4.00am when I was awakened by an orderly who said the Colonel wanted me at once.

Narrator

The Colonel told him that a four-mile gap had appeared in the Allied line. The task of Cosmo's division was to fill it up.

Meanwhile in Chiswick life was becoming more difficult and dangerous. The huge and alarming Zeppelins had already caused hundreds of deaths in Britain.

Zeppelin raid

Lilian

We have had a depressing week of fog and raids. They unshipped over half a dozen bombs between Gunnersbury station and Kew Bridge, but it did no harm to us and missed Brentford Gas works by a few yards. Elizabeth…

Narrator

Lilian's daughter…

Lilian

…has got a nasty shaking and wakes screaming at the slightest noise and refuses to go to sleep or stay in the room alone.

Narrator

Elizabeth was not alone in being scared of the sound of the Zeppelins.

Pictures of Zeppelin damage in London

Although the huge airships were clumsy and vulnerable, they still killed more than 500 people in Britain during the war.

Zeppelin pictures off

Meanwhile out in France Cosmo and his men were trying to plug the four-mile gap in the British lines. When he revised and polished his diary entries, this is how Cosmo described the next, unexpected, stage of the Retreat.

Cosmo

Advance with caution was the order, so my Company was detailed to push out scouts and patrols. Day was breaking as I set off in the thick mist with my Company to get as far forward as possible and into touch with the enemy. There was not a shell nor a bullet to be heard, only an eerie silence. The country was flat and cultivated in places, though it still bore the traces of the great advance in the Somme days. I advanced for about half a mile but found no enemy. We came across three machine gunners from Percy's Division, with their gun, but quite lost and cut off from their units. I sent word back to the Colonel telling him how far we had got and that we could find no enemy. About an hour afterwards I had a message to say that I had to fall back again and provide a rear-guard for the remainder of the battalion which was falling back to a position on the banks of the River Somme. The message was urgent; it was essential that we should move at once. From what I learnt afterwards, the Bosch were pushing up elsewhere and had almost cut us off.

That retirement was one of the most disheartening and tiring events I had ever been through. We trudged across country for miles – all over the battlefields where so many fights had been waged during the Battle of the Somme, over ground which was recovering and assuming a more normal appearance. To add to our discomfort, it was one of the hottest days we had had this year. Eventually we arrived at the River Somme which we crossed at Falvy. The bridge was already mined and ready to be blown at a moment's notice. After a rest we continued our march back to Marchlepot, passing on the way regiments of our cavalry pouring out towards their positions. The wounded were being carried on all manner of stretchers – wire netting, sacking etc. The motor ambulances were full to overflowing; it was a most distressing sight to see all the poor fellows suffering. The sun was very strong, and everyone was whacked to the wide.

Mother

24 March

My dear son

On Friday morning we read of the great offensive and since then have, along with thousands of others, been devouring the newspapers for later dispatches. Last night's gave me a sleepless night – all this perfectly summer-like day we yearn to know what is happening to our sons…

Heaps and heaps of love my very dear son. God bless you. May he keep you safe during this terrible struggle.

Always your affectionate, Mother.

Narrator

The next day Cosmo's company re-joined the remainder of the battalion. The CO sent a message that they must now move forward again to counterattack the Germans.

Shells, then machine gun fire

Cosmo

The country was very flat and open which, in some ways, was rather an advantage. Accordingly, at 10.00am we set off with our tails well up, and only too jolly thankful to move forward for a change. Soon we came under shrapnel fire and so deployed out. After advancing about a mile and a half we ran up against the Bosch and commenced a great fight. There was not much artillery, but there was any amount of rifle and machine gun fire. Our Signals officer got a machine gun bullet through his wrist early on in the proceedings and promptly started his journey to England!! The battle went on for about an hour, but we were up against more than we could manage as we were exposed on our right flank.

Narrator

Another retreat became inevitable, with the Middlesex men letting the Sussex and Northants soldiers go back first. While Cosmo was lying in a field waiting for this to happen, what he calls 'a sad and gruesome' incident occurred.

Sound of an aeroplane diving, then crashing.

Cosmo

One of our aeroplanes appeared; it had been flying over the enemy's lines and was obviously in difficulties. After a moment or two it began to come down nose first and we all thought that he was going to flatten out and land. Very soon, however, it was obvious that the pilot was either unconscious or dead because the plane came rushing down with the engine full on. It hit the ground, nose-first, about thirty yards from me, and immediately, in one puff, became a big flame which continued to burn for about half an hour. Any idea of helping the pilot was out of the question as he must have been killed instantly – if he was not already dead when he hit the ground.

Narrator

Fortunately, the Germans were unable to follow up this Middlesex retreat and Cosmo was able to get his company into an old trench in the village of Punchy. Just before dark he had noticed that the enemy were sending out scouts and reconnoîtring – obviously unaware of the position Cosmo and his men were holding. He waited and listened.

Horses' hooves, men marching.

Cosmo

After about half an hour we could hear large numbers of Bosch on the roads in front. The clatter of horses hooves was as distinct as could be. Also, we could hear large parties of infantry marching along – the tramp, tramp, tramp made one imagine the whole German Army was advancing against my Company. Suddenly the tramping in the distance became louder and louder and we could hear them shouting to each other, "Karl….Companie" It was an anxious moment for me and in fact for us all. Not a man fired a shot though they were anxiously looking at me, as much as to say I was leaving it too late.

After a bit I could hear them coming marching along in column straight down a road leading to our position – shouting out orders and other things which I couldn't understand. When they were about fifty yards away. I gave the order, "Rapid Fire" and we let 'em have it.

Machine gun fire

Every machine gun opened at once and every man fired rapid fire, for three minutes. The silence of a moment before became an ear-splitting roar, and we heard them screaming and scrambling about the woods and bushes.

When I gave the order, "Cease fire" we could hear moans and groans in front and people softly calling. The proud, brazen-faced tactics of marching in column, shouting as they came, had suddenly changed, and I think that little party of Bosch learned to have a wholesome respect for "Rapid Fire" from a bunch of very tired Middlesex men.

Narrator

This was the action which earned Cosmo the Military Cross. Immediately afterwards he was called to a meeting with his CO and those of other battalions in the brigade. They pored over a map by the light of the stump of a candle. The decision was to evacuate, continue the retirement.

Back in Bedford Park they were keeping calm and learning to live with the Zeppelins.

Lilian

Elizabeth seems to be getting over her air-raid shock and is sleeping more quietly – though she still enquires: 'is there is to be an Air Raid tonight, Mummy?' On Wednesday last, Mother, Father and I had a walk from Teddington to Richmond by the river. It was just getting dusk as we got to the brow of the bridge and the grey river and sky and the few twinkles of artificial light looked even more beautiful than in the full sunshine of summer.

On our way we had seen the damage done by the bombs. It was perfectly amazing to see that five bombs, dropped amongst houses and all within an area of 500 yards, should have caused no other damage than holes in the road and numerous broken windows.

Best of love from us all, Lilian.

Cosmo

After the meeting, I arrived back at my line, gathered the platoon commanders together and issued orders. Each officer crept away with his platoon one at a time, while the remainder kept up a desultory fire. I stayed with the Sergeant Major until they were all out and then we crept away with the feeling that about a thousand Bosch were watching all our movements. I expect it seems strange that we repeatedly evacuated positions when there was no apparent need. Whenever we did so it was because the Bosch had attacked and got round us, often miles away to our right and left, and our withdrawing was the order of higher command.

Narrator

The retreat continued the next day as a sizeable German force was still pursuing them. On that day, 26 March, James, with no word from his son, relieved his worry with a letter.

Father

Our newspapers tell of such astounding doings in your part of the world that we are on the tiptoe of anxiety. Patriotic concern looms big in one's mind, but paternal love gives the most acute twinges. We can read how the large battle rolls, but how do our two dear ones fare? We know they are fighting against frightful odds and must be worn out with fatigue… Haunting fears we dare not express lie underneath out thoughts.

Goodnight dear son, with love, Father.

Narrator

The situation remained confused, but the exhausting retreat continued. Cosmo noticed that the Colonel of the Sussex regiment was 'in a dreadful state of nerves, bordering on collapse,' but he had nothing but praise for his own CO, a Colonel Greene who walked about over the top all the time – absolutely regardless of the intense fire from both artillery and machine guns and the fact that his runner was shot dead at his side. Then, on Easter Saturday 1918, something very unlikely happened to Cosmo.

Cosmo

During the afternoon I noticed three or four motorcars coming down the main road from Amiens to Berteaucourt. They stopped and the occupants walked over to my post. One man in a trilby hat I recognised as Winston Churchill. He came towards me and asked if I was in charge of the support line at this point. I told him I was and he continued as follows: "Ah, yes my boy, and what is your name? Here is Monsieur Clemenceau. Come along and I will introduce you to him." I then noticed old Clemenceau who was wearing a large black cape. I saluted, clicked my heels and the old boy shook hands with me. He spoke very good English and asked what sort of time we had had; whether I was tired etc.etc. Then he told us that thousands of French troops were behind us and that thousands of British troops were coming out from England daily. I will never forget his brilliant, shining eyes. They seemed to pierce through one. Churchill gave me some smokes and one of his cigars.

Narrator

Despite the confusion, the retreat had been successful – Allied casualties had been minimised and the attack had petered out. Cosmo summed up his feelings about the retreat like this:

Cosmo

Reading over my diary of the March Retreat, what strikes me most is the number of times, as a Company Commander, I got orders from my superiors to retire. On every occasion we could have fought on and continued to inflict enormous casualties on the enemy. And on every occasion my officers and men wanted to stay and at times grumbled sorely at having to retire. Not through any inborn British valour or similar sterling qualities but because our fatigue was so extreme that lying on the ground and firing at Germans was so much more restful than scrambling with pack and rifle over hard country.

Narrator

By Easter Sunday 1918, Cosmo's family still did not have any news of him.

Ruth

Dearest Cosmo

I am just longing to hear from you, to know that you have come through this hideous week safely. We can never know how terrible it must have been.

Goodnight dear old boy and all my love and sympathy for all you have gone through. Ruth

Narrator

At last a letter came from France.

Cosmo

Mid-day Easter Sunday, 31 March 1918

Dear Mother and Father

What an anxious period without news you must have been going through during the last ten or eleven days. I have sent you a field card whenever it was possible, but I think this only happened twice. I have been fighting since the first day it started and have been through several battles without a scratch. This period has been the most anxious and arduous of all the time I have had in France. During a retirement one of the chief things to fight against is depression. Day after day we have fought and had to retire and march for miles and miles – no sleep and only army biscuits to eat if lucky.

Easter Sunday has brought a great feeling of hope. The sun is shining, and the country is beautiful. I am certain I shall be allowed to come through it all and live to see victory.

Mother

Your letter written on Easter Sunday came tonight. I cannot tell you how delighted and happy it has made us. Think of you being introduced to M. Clemenceau. It has turned much colder tonight. Ruth is at Weymouth with Doris and Colville.

Goodnight my very dear son, bestest love, may God bless you.

Always your affectionate mother, E. Clark.

Narrator

The Middlesex now had support from fresh French troops and, apart from the heavy and continuous rain, and a painful boil on his neck, Cosmo was almost comfortable. The retreat had been distressing and exhausting, but Cosmo's nerve had held.

Mother

6 May 1918, Rustington, Sussex

My dearest son

I am staying down here for a week. Doris has taken a delightful little furnished house and will be here for most of this year. We are only three minutes from the sea and the country around is really pretty. The only blot on the landscape is that the Americans are building a big aerodrome in a field right opposite the house. So the place swarms with Americans, not at all a nice set of men.

Colville has got as far as Gibraltar. He wrote Doris 29 pages, so now she is much happier – she felt his going away terribly.

I have a little news for you: about the end of September Doris expects a dear little baby. Both she and Col are very happy about it.

May God bring you safe through this terrible struggle is the prayer of your devoted mother, E. Clark.

Narrator

Percy's division had been in the thick of it too – taking prisoners from fourteen different German divisions. Percy told his parents the remarkable story of how one of their Battalion commanders had himself been taken prisoner three times in one day – and each time escaped – twice by killing his guard and once by knocking him out with his fists.

Lilian

26 April

Yesterday was so fine that Doris…

Narrator

Who had come up to stay at No. 44…

Lilian

…and I took the three children to Twickenham by tram. The river was very full, over the towpath in places, and looked so beautiful. We sat under the trees by the boathouses while the kiddies did their best to get drowned. Then we walked in the direction of Richmond, but through the grounds of Marble Hill. Doris had never been that way before, and she enjoyed herself as much as the children.

Narrator

Ruth, Ellen and Lilian kept up the flow of letters to Cosmo – Ruth enquiring if he had heard of folk-dancing classes for the Tommies – evidently 50,000 had attended in various camps. There was news that Ellen had had mumps, that father was busy planting beans in his allotment and that they now had a maid with the impressive name of Grantham to help at No. 44. Cosmo's father was anxious to keep up his son's resolve 'in these days of frightful testing.'

Father

One would like to write in a tone of love and pity, but that might soften where we know just hard resolution is needed. Self-pity would be fatal. To break into anger is a parent's right... against those vile spirits of evil who have fastened, as in a vice, these horrors upon the world.

Narrator

Ruth found out a few details of Colville's assignment. He was in command of the trawler 'Thomas Bird' but he could not tell his sister anything about what the ship would do.

Ruth

There is a skipper (v. 'snotty') and a crew of 20. The wardroom is about five feet square, and the most palatial room on the ship is of course Col's – it is 6 feet square. The skipper is supposed to navigate, and Col is responsible for everything. But the skipper is so nervous that Col was on the bridge all the way to Gibraltar – never had his clothes off and had very little sleep. It will be a relief to hear of his safe arrival in Italy – the ship is so tiny, it seems a miracle that it has weathered the Bay of Biscay.

Narrator

James was preoccupied with Cosmo's Somme Retreat diary.

Father

You must not fail to write it up to April 7th. If you don't do it now the incidents will be lost for ever. It is astonishing how one forgets, and should anything happen to you, before it is put down, no one else would ever know! Written down it will be a family heirloom, proudly preserved. Remember it was the biggest battle ever fought. A fifty-mile front! The enemy casualties are calculated at a quarter of a million. It lasted a fortnight.

It sounds rather out of place to say it, but I have just got my new gold plate of upper back teeth put in! Very costly, but a vulcanite one couldn't stand my awful bite, so the dentist said. I have been grinning at Ruth and Lilian to show off. Mother's are not yet finished.

Narrator

The war looked as if it was getting near its end, but the

family kept up the flow of letters to France, specially Ellen with her tales of boarding school life.

Ellen

3 Elfin Road, Fishponds, Bristol

Dearest Cosmo

Last Thursday, our Ascension Day holiday was a simply perfect day – hot and sunny but with a light breeze. We cycled 48 miles to Weston-super-Mare and back. We spent an hour on the sands at Weston and badly wanted to have a donkey ride but were afraid that students might also be down there and as Mrs Pope, the lady superintendent, was with us we had to behave nicely – not that she was a damper on our spirits or fun – far from it, but we didn't do anything wild. I don't think I've ever enjoyed a ride like the one coming back. When you get into Bristol there are three more miles to Fishponds and all up hill, enough to be a fearful drag, especially after 45 miles. But Mrs Pope and I did it, the other two took the tram.

Father

Mother and I went to see the American soldiers march to Waterloo from Wellington barracks. It was a great occasion. They are not the least bit of the type I expected to see. One imagines, lean, long, tough young

Uncle Sams. They are fat, short in the leg, big-bottomed fellows. Hefty, beefy, determined men, excellent fighting material surely, but of very unspiritual countenance and underdeveloped soul.

Cosmo

30 June, France

My dear Mother and Father

It has been glorious today – very hot and the sun shining all day. Horsford and I went round the line this afternoon and gathered up a big bunch of cornflowers and poppies to decorate the dug-out. Wildflowers abound everywhere – they are almost as abundant as the rats and mice!

Narrator

For Cosmo the summer of 1918 was very much quieter than the spring had been – he was sent on courses and then un-sent, he played tennis at a very luxurious billet, he fraternised a little with French soldiers. The war, with General Foch now in charge of the allied forces, was, at last, going well. But the Clarks didn't stop writing to each other.

Ellen

Dearest Cosmo

So you have been having a dose of Spanish Flu – it's simply raging in this country. London has half its schools closed according to the papers. So far, it has not attacked Bristol. I only hope we don't get it at the Flax Camp. The latest about the camp is that we are going to Wellington in Somerset and we are to be camped in a cricket field. Today is the last day of term. I am sitting supervising an exam and after that we have a grand tea, which is supposed to be given by the staff to the girls, and then a dance. There will be great doings tonight, not one will dream of going to bed before 2.00am and they are allowed to make as much noise as they like.

Narrator

Ellen got to her flax camp where they were paid to work. Later she was joined by Ruth – and her parents, who dropped in after a quite arduous walking holiday. James noted that 'the new style of college girl is a delightful surprise to the old-fashioned country folk'.

Father

I must write a line tonight. Your last letter said you were to move the next day to be 'in it'.

On Tuesday morning I awoke at 4.00am for some unexplained reason and had you very much in mind until I got up at 6 o'clock. Your letter arrived the evening after. I wonder what you were about on Tuesday 8th at 4.00am? Sound asleep, I hope…

Narrator

James's premonitions were a bit uncanny, as he soon found out.

Loud shell explosion

The very next day Cosmo was wounded again.

Cosmo

I expect by now you will have either heard from the War Office or received my postcard to say I have been hit. I have got a clean bullet wound through my right leg, between ankle and calf. No bones broken. I am very lucky, as the German who shot me was only twenty yards away. Fortunately, he was a bad shot. Tomorrow I am being sent to Blighty, so will probably get there before this letter.

Narrator

So Cosmo's war was over in October 1918. He was well on his way to recovery when the struggle finally ended a month later. He was well enough to hobble along to the first Armistice Day service on 11 November, 1918.

Afterwards crowds made way for the veteran on crutches in the crowded tube station.

Over the next few years, he recovered fully and trained to be the artist he wanted to be.

Cosmo painting of officers in dugout

He became an excellent painter and, ultimately, a very able arts administrator. This is how he remembered one of his warmer billets in France.

In 1922 Cosmo met another art student at the Royal Academy school – Jean Wymer.

Painting off. Picture of Jean Wymer on.

She thought he looked unhappy and was sure that this was the effect of the war. They married in 1924 and Jean also became a painter of quality. Much, much later, their daughter Julia excavated the family's old tin trunk. It contained, mouldering but decipherable, the letters you have just heard.

Jean Wymer picture off

Cosmo survived but, as with many veterans, there was a price to pay. The painful memories of the trenches – of, for example, a friend eating breakfast with him one moment, blown to pieces the next – were in his mind for the rest of his life, but at least he had the ability to talk about them.

In the terrible stresses of the trenches deep friendships had formed. As he recovered, Cosmo wrote to Sergeant Major Sandoe who had been through many desperate moments with him. He got this touching reply, written in France where Sandoe was still serving. He had been delighted to hear that his captain was recovering.

Cosmo

(reading the letter)

It came as a blow to me when I left you on the stretcher to be carried away. As soon as I saw you going towards the machine gun post I thought you were going too far, only it wasn't for me to tell you, only that it was my duty to pull you through in case you might be killed.

Well sir, the Bosch shelled for a long time to try to get us away from the sunken road, but we hung on to the last. We got relieved about 3 o'clock the same day. Yes sir, it was rather hard luck that I didn't get the MC, but I'm satisfied with what I got, something to look at in time to come. Dear sir, I should have liked to have gone forward instead of coming back, as I shall never have another chance again.

I hope you will soon get better and may good luck follow you in the near future, also wishing you a Merry Christmas.

Yours sincerely

S.H. Sandoe

P.S. I should like to hear from you when time permits.

Narrator

Cosmo had very strong feelings of loyalty to the Tommies under his command. What happened when he was asked to be a 'Prisoner's Friend' towards the end of the war was so painful that he was hardly able to talk about it.

Cosmo leads in the young prisoner during the next speech. They sit at the end of a long table – prisoner facing audience, Cosmo at his side. There are three unfilled chairs – one at each side of the table and one at the top, facing the prisoner.

Narrator

In the spring of 1918 David Stevenson was a young private in the Middlesex who was court-martialled for desertion. Cosmo, who had no legal training, was there for him at the trial.

Stevenson's company had just come out of the trenches. The young Scottish soldier, had been hoping for leave – he hadn't had it for a year. When he found out it had been cancelled, he went for a long, meandering walk.

The court martial was held at Bully Grenay, close to the mining town of Bully les Mines.

The Prisoner

I don't know what came over me for the moment, but I went too far from my unit, so I went on till I got to Mons.

Narrator

Cosmo's task in representing Stevenson was not made easier by the fact that the young Scotsman – he was 22 – had deserted his unit for some weeks and he had a long history of offences – chiefly going AWOL, being drunk and disorderly and malingering.

Cosmo and the Prisoner shift in their chairs to face one of the empty chairs

Major Hingley, one of his commanding officers:

Hingley

(Pre-recorded voice over)

Stevenson is undependable, unreliable, except that in the face of any danger he can be relied on to run away.

Narrator

Lieutenant General Aylmer Hunter made his contribution:

Hunter

(Pre-recorded voice over)

The trouble with Stevenson is his obvious and habitual tendency to defy all authority.

Cosmo

Addressing the 'judge's' chair at the top end of the table

I would like you to consider the question of David Stevenson's mental health. He has not had leave for a year; it is not difficult to imagine how disappointed he must have been. And he did not resist arrest, although he knew well the likely punishment for desertion. I question his grip on reality. He is young, he is confused, he is a poor soldier – I'm sorry to say, of little use to the regiment. He needs to be excluded, disgraced, sent home, perhaps given treatment. But it is my belief that we should *not* put him in the same category as our enemies. He has not served us well, but I must ask the court not to impose the ultimate penalty.

Narrator

We do not know *exactly* what Cosmo said to the court or the prisoner, but the court papers record a crushing judgement by the senior officer

All eyes and attention focus on empty chair at the top of the table

The 'Judge'

(Pre-recorded voice over)

Stevenson has been an undisciplined member of a disciplined Battalion. Such an example is bad for young men now serving. I regret I have no recommendation for mercy to submit and I therefore consider the sentence of death should be carried out.

Narrator

His view was endorsed by no less a person than Field Marshal Haig himself who wrote just a laconic 'confirmed' on the paperwork.

Stevenson was shot at dawn on July 18, 1918.

A melancholy tune begins and continues quietly under the narration

The sergeant in charge of the firing squad knew him.

Many of the men who had been ordered to shoot their colleague were nervous – and found it difficult to fire. The last words the lad from Glasgow said, according to the sergeant in charge of the firing squad, were, 'What will my mother say?' We can be fairly sure Cosmo would have wanted to save the young man, however unreliable, from execution. After all Cosmo had himself felt fear and a strong desire to leave the battlefields, but – through good fortune, family support and his native grit – he had managed to overcome those fears.

Music ends

By the end of the Great War, at the age of 21, Cosmo Clark had become an accomplished, battle-hardened soldier.

He had played his part in two great historic battles and many smaller ones, but the moments before action were always painful. Reflecting in his Retreat Diary he wrote about the fearful anticipation he felt as a company commander, in charge of four officers and a hundred and twenty men, when an attack was expected.

Cosmo

One's feeling on occasions like this were very strange and very disconcerting. At intervals I pictured the spectacle of hordes of Germans assaulting our trenches and the chances

of their gaining a footing. Then the possibilities of death –
a somewhat gruesome thing to talk about now, but at the
time a thing which seemed very possible if not probable.
Have I disposed my men and machine guns and officers in
the best way possible, both from the point-of-view of their
welfare and the best position for them to inflict casualties?
Questions like these keep asserting themselves. Last, but
by no means least, comes the awful series of misdeeds and
sins of one's career – they assume gigantic sizes and won't
leave one's mind – any idea of forgiveness of such things is
out of the question. So, you see it's not all beer and skittles
awaiting the Hun's offensive. The trials and tribulations of
imagination and anticipation are infinitely worse than the
actual fighting.

Narrator

Cosmo Clark was a lucky survivor. None of his three
wounds was serious; and both he and his family escaped
Spanish Flu. He had risked his life, but fate did not require
of him the Great Sacrifice made by millions of others.

His paintings, his happy marriage to Jean, and his
daughter Julia, who wrote childrens' books and married
the musician Stephen Rhys and was much loved in
the parish of Christ Church, East Sheen, provide the

happy ending to this story of Cosmo's War. Now as a small tribute to Cosmo and all those who served and died in the Great War, here is a piece of music Cosmo specially loved.

A suitable piece is played on the piano, perhaps Claire de Lune by Debussy or Chanson de Matin by Elgar.

Cosmo's mature drawings and paintings are screened for the duration.

Callen Ri

Origins

The letters which are the raw material of this play were collected and edited by Cosmo's wife Jean and published by his daughter Julia Rhys. Here is the foreword to The Tin Trunk, *written by Julia.*

The tin trunk is battered and travel stained. My mother said she kept her treasures in it when she was a child. One day she found her things turned out on the floor; her brother had needed a case to pack, like Cosmo, when he joined the fighting in France. Mercifully, much later, the soldier brother returned, bringing the trunk with him. His young sister grew up and met and married another survivor of that war, Cosmo Clark. The trunk was filled with other precious things, locked up and stored for a very long time. At last, some time after my father died, when she was in her eighties, my mother decided to open the trunk and look through the contents. Stored inside were letters and drawings from those years and before she died my mother began to read and choose some of the letters; she wanted to make them into a book.

Like most of the other soldiers, my father wrote home to his family every few days. Unlike so many, he was not killed, so the trunk held the whole story of his war. The drawings he posted home were mostly from his first year in France, but his letters go on until October 1918. He wrote from dugouts, under fire, during battles or while coping with enforced and baffling inactivity. Having to censor his own mail, hardly any part of the line is named, few towns are disclosed and most battles are anonymous. For anyone interested, almost all can be traced with a little detective work and some reference to Western Front and regimental history.

The trunk held other letters and even small drawings, by parents, sisters, brothers and friends. My father valued them so much then and they help our understanding of that time now, so some are included here. These letters have greetings and signatures included, but those from my father, except for the first and last, are left without; he is after all, telling one story.

People were really generous with their time and skills in helping with my mother's project. I do want to thank Olive Playle for her long and exacting task in typing the originals. Sidney Hutchinson has written such a very thoughtful introduction. Malcolm Brown and Nigel Steel, from the Imperial War Museum have given much help and advice. Julian Putkowski was very generous in sharing his research and the estate of Sir Winston Churchill kindly gave permission to print an extract from his memoirs. My cousin John Clark, son of Percy, the elder officer brother who gave my father so much support, provided information and family history. Our daughter Annabel has worked really hard on design and layout and my husband Stephen as always, has provided endless encouragement.

Few of us now have met anything like the experiences that follow but most of our revulsion against war springs from that time. Like millions of others a neighbour and I have protested, vigiled and walked for peace together. Her father also fought courageously in that war; he was German. So now I read and re-read one particular letter written in winter from the trenches when my father was just nineteen. That was the time when he risked a few moments of fun and found amongst the enemy, for just those moments, a friend.

(The Tin Trunk was first published in 2000 by F.S. & J. Rhys)

The **Tin Trunk**

Letters and Drawings 1914-1918
COSMO CLARK

POST OFFICE TELEGRAPHS.

Office Stamp.

LONDON
3
OC 14
16
O.H.S

led in at	Office of Origin and Service Instructions	Words	Charges to pay
30	Dover D.	29	

THIS FORM MUST ACCOMPANY ANY ENQUIRY RESPECTING THIS TELEGRAM.

Received here at .M.

Clark 44 Rusthall Avenue Bedford. Park W

arrived at dover tonight bullet wound wound right leg very slight being sent to holmwood in sussex will wire you again tomorrow Cosmo

---

POST CARD

The Address only to be Written Here

Have got a wait of about two hours here so am looking round the town. The sea looks uncannily choppy Cosmo

Mr & Mrs J. Clark
44 Rusthall Avenue
Bedford Park
London W

Above: Cosmo married Jean Wymer in 1924
Overleaf: The Dugout, 1920 by Cosmo Clark, 28cm x 42cm

Post War, what happened to...

Cosmo

He was 21 when the war ended. Recovering from his wounds, he went back briefly to Goldsmith's College to continue his art education. Then he went to Paris and studied at the Académie Julian. Next, he enrolled at the Royal Academy School of Painting – where he excelled, winning both a gold medal and a travelling scholarship.

It was while he was there that he met the nineteen-year-old Jean Wymer, who had already studied at the Sidcup School of Art. When they met there was an instant affinity and they married in 1924, soon spending time travelling in France and later, in 1926, lodging near a Leicestershire colliery, making drawings of the miners. Before the end of the decade, they had done a year in New York and then come home to St Peter's Square in Hammersmith where their daughter Julia was born.

Both Cosmo and Jean continued to paint and teach throughout the 1930s. Cosmo was one of the artists chosen to illustrate T.E. Lawrence's *Seven Pillars of Wisdom* and Jean spent time in Sickert's studio. In 1938 Cosmo was made head of Hackney School of Art. But another war was about to break out. Cosmo was soon employed as Chief Camouflage officer at the Ministry of Home Security. This he did till 1942, based in Leamington Spa. He and Jean had to manage what little private work they did in a small barn which was very open to the elements.

Then life changed again: Cosmo was appointed Director of the Rural Industries Bureau. The job suited him admirably and for more than twenty years his enthusiasm and knowledge of country crafts, allied to his administrative ability, drove the Bureau forward. Eventually he set up a new headquarters at Wimbledon Common which was, to quote Cosmo's friend, Sidney Hutchison: 'in the post-war years, the pre-eminent advisory centre for the traditional smaller industries of the countryside.'

Cosmo was delighted that his daughter Julia wrote children's books and she and her husband, the musician Stephen Rhys, produced six grandchildren. Cosmo was much in demand on committees, but he went on finding time to paint his street scenes (especially open-air markets and cafes), often done at night, and sporting events (particularly cycling and boxing). Jean remained versatile and undertook several big mural projects. Cosmo died at his Hammersmith home in 1967 at the age of 70; Jean survived him by 32 years.

Above: Mells Village Shop, by Jean Clark, 1954 (49 x 75cm)
(Photo credit: RWA - Royal West of England Academy)

Overleaf: English Country Fair, (Stokenchurch, Buckinghamshire)
by Cosmo Clark, 1933 (102 x 127cm)

What happened to...
the rest of the Clarks?

James and Elizabeth celebrated their Diamond Wedding on 20th April 1942 at Ellen's house in Reigate. All their surviving children were present. James died peacefully the following January and Elizabeth 10 years later at the age of 96. James had continued to paint until he was in his 80s.

Percy married Dorothy Foulgar in 1920. She was a friend and colleague of his sister Ruth at the Chelsea College. They had four children and numerous grandchildren and great grandchildren. Percy remobilised into the Royal Engineers in 1919 and had a very successful military career. He served in India and Iraq and was awarded the CBE for his work in France during the Second World War.

Colville had married Doris Briscoe in 1918 and they settled in South Africa. He returned to the Merchant Navy where he had been apprenticed. He died in 1931 and afterwards his eldest daughter Joan came to live with James and Elizabeth in Bedford Park.

Lilian had married John Goodchild in 1909. John was a clergyman and Lilian taught art, painted very successfully and raised four children. In 1927 they moved to Brington, Huntingdonshire, and then to Cambridge. 'Little Cosmo' studied at Reading, joined the army but was invalided out. After a long illness he died in 1947.

Ruth had joined the staff of the Chelsea College of Physical Education in 1915, where she had trained originally. She taught there and was the Deputy Principal for many years. Neither she nor her younger sister, Ellen, married, but they travelled extensively together.

Ellen taught art and the craft of bookbinding at many schools – ending up as Deputy Principal of the Girls High School in Reigate. She built a house in the town where she looked after her parents in their later years. Ellen was also the proud owner of a motorbike.

The Old Bridge, Huntingdon, by Lilian Clark, 1926 (25 x 15in)

* Biographical information kindly supplied by Janice Goodchild
(Grandaughter of Lilian Clark)

Author

Bernard Adams is keen to remind readers of this play that most of it was written by the Clark family of Rusthall Avenue, Chiswick. The letters, going to and from the trenches for nearly three years, from 1915 to 1918, made rich raw material. Editing them into a chronological narrative was one of the most enjoyable tasks of his writing life.

He was born in Dublin in 1939, but for much of his career was a journalist and television producer based in London. In 2001 Lilliput Press published his life of Denis Johnston, Irish dramatist and BBC war correspondent. Since then, he has written three dramas – one of which, *Killing Hitler*, about the July 1944 plot to assassinate the Führer, went on at the O'Reilly theatre in Oxford. His most recent play, *Harry Gleeson*, is about a Tipperary man, falsely accused of a murder, and hanged in 1941 for a crime he did not commit. And a biography of Mary O'Malley, founder of the embattled Lyric Theatre, Belfast, is due out now.

Designer

Annie Davis designed this book, with ease due to the incredible content provided from many sources, particularly Bernard Adams, but also from John F. F. Clark's, *The Life of James Clark* (shortly to be republished). Her love for painting and design came from Cosmo's wife, (her grandmother), Jean Clark (RWS, NEAC), who moved to Suffolk shortly after Cosmo died and continued to paint the beautiful countryside well into her 90s.

She is forever grateful to Bernard, and also Torin Douglas for taking such an interest in James Clark and his family, helping to unearth all kinds of interesting and previously unknown information.

Annie has designed and self-published a few books including one by her mother Julia Rhys, *The Paintbrush* (2013 – Published F.S. & J. Rhys), which is a very good read and includes biographical elements of Cosmo and Jean's life as artists in the inter-war years.